# Angelic Dreams
## Bedtime Healing Meditation for Children

Little Blue Zen

# Angelic Dreams

## Copyright@ 2024 Jo Galloway

The right of the author has been asserted to her following the copyright writing, designs and patent act of Australia.

All rights reserved. No part of this book may be reproduced, stored or transmitted by any means whether auditory, graphic, mechanical, or electronic without the written permission of the author. Unauthorised reproduction of any part of this work is illegal and is punishable by law.

Unless otherwise noted, the author and the publisher make no explicit guarantees as the accuracy of the information contained in this book may differ based on individual experiences and context

ISBN: 978-1-7635801-8-3

Published by Little Blue Zen

Birdwood NSW

Printed in Australia

Cover Design: Gagan Karunachandra

Editing: Kristine Gibson

jo@littlebluezen.com

http://www.littlebluezen.com

# Angelic Dreams

## Bedtime Healing Meditation for Children

## Jo Galloway

**Your child may like other books in this series**

- Bully Proof. Keeping out the bullies.

- I am Different, I am Me.

- The Magical Treasure Hunt. Building Confidence.

- The Magical Worry Balloon.

- I Love School.

- Scared of the Dark.

- Bedwetting, Dry Nights.

- A Coat of Flying Colours

# INTRODUCTION

## Why Healing Meditations.

As children we make sense of our experiences based on our limited understanding and perception. We may misinterpret events or draw conclusions that form the basis of limiting beliefs that influence our entire life. These beliefs become ingrained over time, shaping our thoughts, feelings and behaviours well into adulthood unless consciously challenged.

In my work as a practising Hypnotherapist, I've found that all my clients' concerns, whether rooted in fears, feelings of inadequacy, addictive behaviours, or other challenges, trace back to their early childhood experiences, interactions, and upbringing. It's important to note that these issues don't exclusively stem from abusive or dysfunctional environments; limiting beliefs can arise from various circumstances.

Parents or caregivers wield substantial influence in shaping our perceptions of ourselves and the world around us. Remarks, criticisms, or comparisons made by family members can foster beliefs about our capabilities, worthiness, or potential. Furthermore, interactions with peers, teachers, and authority figures also contribute to the formation of these beliefs. Repeated experiences of rejection or failure can solidify beliefs such as "I'm not good enough" or "I'm unworthy of love."

This realization ignited my passion for intervening at the source: working with children to prevent these beliefs from taking root and manifesting into significant challenges in adulthood. By addressing issues early on, we can guide children to develop into the best versions of themselves, free from the burden of limiting beliefs that could otherwise dominate their lives.

## How Healing Meditation will help your child.

Teaching children meditation offers a multitude of benefits that can positively influence their daily lives and overall development. A regular mindfulness meditation practice provides valuable tools for managing stress, navigating emotions, and promoting overall well-being. Healing meditations, in particular, bolster your child's self-belief, helping to remove any resistance they may face in adulthood. This leads to a happier, more successful and fulfilling life.

Unlike traditional meditation, which often centres on relaxation, healing meditations go a step further by focusing on recovery, balance, and reprogramming a child's self-belief. These meditations use techniqucs such as breathing exercises, visualization, and guided imagery to not only foster deep relaxation but also reshape their mindset.

This targeted approach helps build a stronger sense of self-confidence and resilience. By integrating positive affirmations and emotional healing, healing meditations offer a distinct advantage over traditional methods, laying a powerful foundation for a child's future success and well-being.

Meditation can also be an effective part of your child's bedtime routine, helping to calm the mind and prepare the body for restful sleep. Techniques like guided imagery and deep breathing, as outlined in this book, can signal to the brain that it's time to wind down.

Sharing these calming moments at bedtime not only strengthens the bond between parent and child, but also creates a supportive and nurturing environment. It also sets a positive example, emphasizing the importance of self-care and mindfulness.

With patience and consistency, you can help your child develop a lifelong practice that supports their mental, emotional, and physical health. Give your child the gift of relaxation and imagination with this easy-to-read story designed to inspire and uplift.

# Angelic Dreams

Angelic Dreams: is a tender and soothing bedtime meditation designed to help children drift peacefully to sleep. This enchanting guide takes little ones on a calming journey with their very own Guardian Angel. As they settle into their cozy beds, they are gently guided through relaxing breathing exercises and imaginative visualization.

The story begins with a comforting routine of deep breaths and relaxation, leading to a magical encounter with a loving Angel. This Guardian Angel, adorned in a glittering golden cape, presents a special gift—a magical sleepy coat—that envelops the child in warmth and tranquility. The coat, described as softer than a bunny's fur and as warm as a loved one's embrace, ensures a night of restful sleep and sweet dreams.

With gentle narration, children are encouraged to feel safe, loved, and protected as they drift off into a world of magical dreams.

This meditation not only helps ease the transition to sleep but also instils a sense of comfort and security that can soothe bedtime anxieties. Perfect for creating a peaceful bedtime routine, Angelic Dreams: offers a serene path to restful sleep and enchanting nighttime adventures.

Delivered in a slow, monotone voice, this story captivates and soothes. ANGELIC DREAMS, is also available on YouTube, providing a soothing auditory experience children can enjoy at home, in the car, or anywhere they need a moment of relaxation."

**Listen on YouTube**

# Angelic Dreams

Hello, my gorgeous little Starlight.

Are you ready for a wonderful adventure?

Ready for a touch of magic?

First, settle into your warm, cozy bed.

Pull up the covers and have a little wiggle.

Find the perfect spot.

Make yourself really comfortable.

Uncross your legs and gently place your hands by your sides.

When you're ready, laying nice and still, softly close your eyes.

Beautiful!

Take a slow, deep breath in through your nose, as if you are smelling a beautiful flower.

Now breathe out your mouth, like you are blowing out all your birthday candles, having a big sigh.

Ahhhhh..........That's right.

As you breathe out, you can feel your body sinking down into your warm, cozy bed.

You're becoming sleepier and sleepier.

So, let's do that again, shall we?

Take another deep breath in, push your tummy out.

Hold your breath, now slowly breathe out.

Sinking down, drifting down, your body is melting down.

You feel your body becoming all floppy and floaty.

Your head rest comfortably on your soft pillow and your body is relaxing like a puppet.

Your cozy warm bed holds you like a cuddle.

You feel so warm and safe.

Bring your thoughts back to your tummy as you breathe in, then breathe out.

You breathe in; you breathe out.

Your head is relaxing as sleepy is coming to you.

Your eyes are so heavy and tired as sleepy is coming to you.

Your arms are so heavy as sleepy is coming to you.

Your legs are so heavy as sleepy is moving through you.

A sleepy feeling is now all over your body, from the top of your head to the very tips of your toes.

You love bedtime - it's your favourite time of the day.

It's a magical place where you can have wonderful dreams.

Sleep is so important; we all need sleep.

Just like we need water to drink, air to breathe and food to eat.

Can you remember back when you were just a tiny little baby?

You could fall asleep anywhere, so easily, all by yourself.

Did you know that all boys and girls have the most wonderful imaginations, way better than grown-ups?

So, you can see perfectly well with your eyes closed.

So, I want you to picture in your brilliant imagination, you can see a light off in the distance.

A beautiful, bright golden light.

It sparkles with moondust and simmers with starlight.

It's comforting, pretty and feels warm and friendly.

This light is slowly drifting towards you.

It's getting closer and closer with every breath you take.

It's still quite a distance away, but you can see it clearly with your eyes closed.

Within the light, you can see a person.

I wonder who it might be...

As the light comes closer, you can see a lady, and she is smiling at you.

You can see she has something on her back.

Whatever it is, it's fluffy—no, it's feathery!

Oh, those must be her wings.

Wow!

This is my Angel, my very own Guardian Angel.

She tells me that all little boys and girls have their own special Angel who visits them at night in their dreams, their magical dreams.

She gracefully floats towards you with her arms outstretched, making you feel so loved by her presence.

You feel safe, bubbling with happiness, wrapped in a special, warm feeling of Angel love.

She smells wonderful too, like strawberry bubble-gum.

Your Angel is standing right in front of you now.

You can even reach out and touch her.

She is incredibly beautiful and very tall.

Taller than Mummy or Daddy, and is wrapped in a golden cape that is all glittery and sparkly.

Her golden light is dazzling.

A halo of magic rainbow mist surrounds her.

She looks into your eyes, and you can feel her love.

Ooh, look! Your Angel has a gift for you.

Her hands are outstretched, offering you a beautiful present.

I wonder what it could be.

You can see it clearly now.

It's a box wrapped in a big red ribbon, shimmering with moonbeams and sparkling with gold dust.

You're so excited, you just love gifts.

You reach out your hands and graciously accept the box with the red ribbon.

Your eyes twinkle with excitement and gratitude as you thank your Guardian Angel.

Eagerly, you untie the ribbon, excited to see what is inside.

You open the box and the gift glides out.

Oh, but what could it be you wonder?

You feel very sleepy and begin to yawn.

You hear your Angel talking.

You lean in to listen as she is talking so softly, so not wake you.

You hear the word 'coat' quietly in your mind.

Words are not coming from your mouth or hers, like when mummy or daddy speak to you.

You are communicating with your Angel in a special silent way.

A secret way between you and your Angel.

You can feel how loving and caring your Angel friend is.

She absolutely adores you.

You're her favourite person in the whole wide world.

She is always with you.

Her gift to you is a very special one, with magical superpowers.

She tells you this is your very own magical sleepy coat.

You gently lift the coat from the box.

It is the most beautiful coat you have ever seen.

It feels incredibly soft, even softer than a bunny rabbit's fur.

It's nicer than a friend's smile, as warm as Mommy's love, and as safe as Daddy's arms.

This coat is super special, like God made it himself, made just for you.

Your Guardian Angel asks you to put it on.

As you wrap the coat around your shoulders, it drapes over you like a cuddle.

This magical sleepy coat completely envelops you as a powerful wave of sleepiness settles over you and through you.

Your coat fits you like Cinderella's slipper.

It was made especially just for you, and it knows exactly what you need.

It is made up of all your favourite colours.

Your Guardian Angel is again talking to you.

She says, "put the hood over your head."

This is a magical sleeping hood protecting you throughout the night, holding in your dreams.

You gently begin falling into a deep, restful slumber of clouds.

Pillows of soft cotton wool envelop you.

Your magical coat wraps you up, calms you, stills you.

Your eyes feel like weights, heavy, droopy, drowsy, almost impossible to open.

You are feeling so happy and so loved.

You just love bedtime.

Bedtime is now your favourite time of the day.

It's a special time where you get to talk with your Angel.

Your Angel tells you she is always with you even when you are awake.

She is always there to help you; all you need to do is ask.

You don't use your human voice when you are talking together.

Instead, you hear her softly inside your mind.

You ask her what her name is.

She is whispering something to you.

You lean in to listen because she is speaking so softly.

She is telling you her name, so be still and listen.

You feel so loved and special because you have your very own Guardian Angel.

Your Guardian Angel knows it's now time for sleep to come.

Your Angel says, "I will stay with you every night."

She curls up at the end of your bed, blowing sweet dream kisses to you, like a unicorn wind on a soft, warm summer breeze.

Happy thoughts and sleepy feelings lay down on you like a warm, comfortable blanket.

Your beautiful magical coat of slumber holds all your dreams in place.

Loving and protecting you as you drift into a wonderful sleep.

Staying asleep all night long, until the morning light.

Sleep now, my beautiful Little Starlight.

Rest deeply and let yourself drift away.

As you dream the most amazing, magical dreams, your coat of sleepy love surrounds you now and always.

Your Guardian Angel is with you, watching over and protecting you all night long.

So, goodnight.

Sweet dreams, my Little Starlight.

Sleep tight..........

# More by Jo Galloway

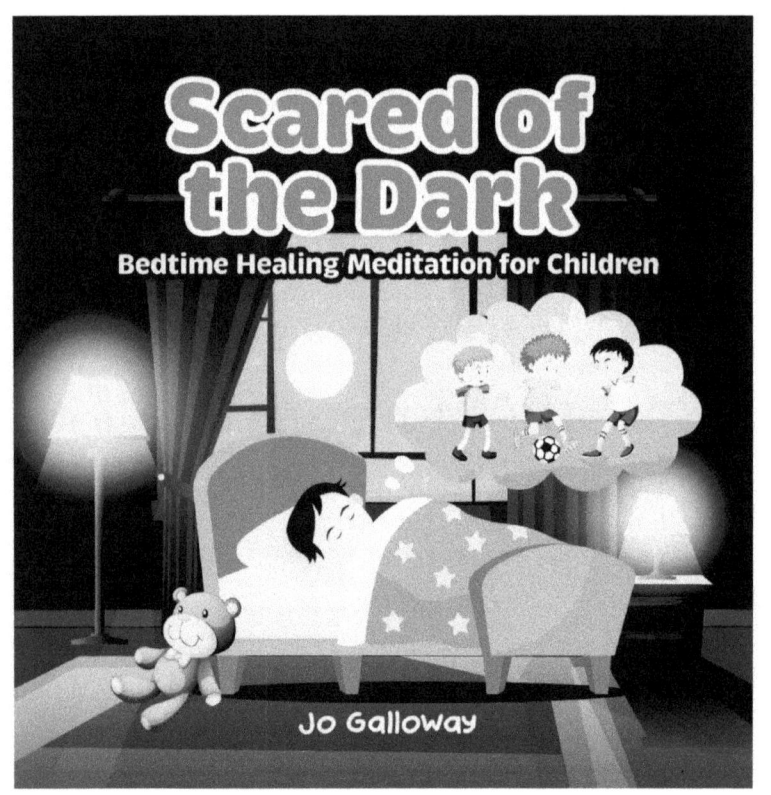

Join Teddy, your brave and comforting friend, on a magical bedtime journey designed to help little ones conquer their fears of the dark. In this gentle Healing Meditation, Teddy shares a heartwarming story about overcoming nighttime worries and using the power of your imagination to transform fear into bravery. Through soothing guidance, deep breathing and a comforting countdown, Teddy helps children relax deeply and embrace their inner courage. Ideal for easing bedtime anxieties, this meditation fosters a sense of safety and confidence, ensuring a peaceful, restful night's sleep.

## Bedwetting, Dry Nights

Dry Nights is a soothing bedtime meditation designed to help children aged 3 to 7 wake up to a dry bed each morning. This gentle and magical story uses comforting language and imagery to empower young listeners to reconnect their brain and bladder, fostering better control and confidence throughout the night.

As children drift off to sleep, gentle reminders reassure them of their newfound ability to stay dry all night, no matter where they sleep. The story ends with a comforting affirmation of their success and control, ensuring that each night is a step towards waking up happy and dry.

# Little Blue Zen.com

Little Blue Zen